Original title:
Flickering Wisps Beneath the Fae Rime

Copyright © 2025 Swan Charm
All rights reserved.

Author: Paula Raudsepp
ISBN HARDBACK: 978-1-80559-470-3
ISBN PAPERBACK: 978-1-80559-969-2

Veils of Light in the Icy Breath

In the stillness, dawn unfolds,
Veils of light in icy breath,
Whispers dance on sparkling cold,
Nature's cloak hides quiet death.

Shadows stretch across the ground,
Silent footprints, soft and rare,
Echoes of the night unbound,
Twinkling gems in frosty air.

Glistening branches catch the gold,
Fractal patterns, beauty's thread,
Stories of the brave and bold,
In the silence, we are led.

Frozen rivers gently flow,
Reflecting dreams of yesteryear,
Secrets that the winds may know,
Carried softly, crystal clear.

In this realm of hush and light,
Time stands still, a breathless pause,
Nature's heart, so pure and bright,
In her arms, we feel the cause.

Wistful Whispers of the Frosted Pines

Amidst the pines, a soft breeze sighs,
Wistful whispers weave through trees,
Memories drape like autumn skies,
In the hush, the spirit frees.

Frosted needles, sharp and fine,
Catch the sunlight, gleam and gleam,
Stories linger, intertwine,
In this tranquil, timeless dream.

Echoes of the past resound,
Rustling leaves, a gentle song,
Nature's pulse a heartbeat found,
Calling souls to wander long.

Snowflakes twirl, a ballet bright,
Painting earth in white embrace,
In this magic, pure delight,
Captures time, a fleeting space.

In the stillness, find your peace,
Listen close, the pines will tell,
Of love's warmth and sweet release,
In their shadows, we dwell well.

Glimmers of the Otherworld

In whispers soft, the shadows call,
Glimmers bright where spirits fall.
A dance of light in the twilight haze,
Where echoes linger in twilight's maze.

Beneath the moon's gentle, glowing glance,
Flittering souls begin their dance.
Through the veil of time they weave,
A tapestry of dreams, we believe.

Radiance Danced Along the Frosted Boughs

A shimmer sparkles on branches bare,
Radiance twirls in the crisp, cold air.
Frosty fingers, a delicate lace,
Embracing silence, a winter's grace.

Each breath of wind sings a soft tune,
Kissed by the light of the silver moon.
Nature's whisper, a gentle sigh,
In stillness, the night birds cry.

Celestial Glows in Darkened Forests

Among the trees where shadows lie,
Celestial glows in the night sky.
Stars peek through an ancient grove,
Illuminating secrets long roved.

The silver beams on the forest floor,
Guide the weary to an unseen door.
Magic stirs in the cool night air,
Awakening dreams that linger there.

Secrets Wrapped in Winter's Embrace

In the embrace of winter's chill,
Secrets hide, quiet and still.
Snowflakes dance in a swirling flight,
Each twirl a tale of the night.

Frozen whispers on the breeze,
Tell of wonders beneath the trees.
In every flake, a story waits,
In winter's realm, the heart elates.

Secrets Adrift in Ethereal Light

In whispers soft, the shadows play,
With secrets lost, they drift away.
A shimmer glows, a fleeting spark,
In twilight's realm, the silence hark.

Veils of mist and luster bright,
Reveal the dreams that take to flight.
In gentle hands, the stories fold,
Of ancient truths yet to be told.

The stars align, their paths entwined,
In silent vows, the heart will find.
Adrift on waves of endless night,
The secrets dance in ethereal light.

Dances of the Winter Spirits

Snowflakes swirl in the frosty air,
Whispering tales with gentle care.
The spirits twirl in winter's grace,
Embracing all in their soft embrace.

Branches creak in the chilling breeze,
While shadows play beneath the trees.
In icy paths, they glide and spin,
The dance of joy, where dreams begin.

Fires crackle, warm and bright,
As echoes of laughter fill the night.
With every step, the world is still,
In winter's heart, a timeless thrill.

Echoes of Celestial Dreams

Beneath the stars, the night ignites,
Whispers of dreams in cosmic flights.
Celestial beings weave through time,
In harmony, their voices chime.

Galaxies swirl in endless dance,
Inviting souls to take a chance.
Each echo sings of love's embrace,
Carving paths in the vastness of space.

The moonlight spills on velvet skies,
Where hopes are born and never die.
In quiet realms, the dreams unite,
In echoes soft, they find their light.

Phantoms in the Frost's Embrace

In winter's grip, the phantoms glide,
Through fields of white, they softly bide.
Their laughter hides in the moonlit haze,
As shadows dance in chilling ways.

Each breath a cloud in the frosty air,
With silken threads, they weave a snare.
In whispered steps, the night unfolds,
A tale of warmth amidst the cold.

The frost encases secrets deep,
In shivers, memories softly creep.
Through timeless halls, the echoes trace,
The phantoms play in winter's embrace.

Glimmers of Enchantment

In the twilight's gentle sway,
Stars awaken, start to play.
A silver mist begins to rise,
Painting magic 'neath the skies.

Glimmers dance on whispered sighs,
Where the heart of longing lies.
A secret well of dreams untold,
Awaits the brave, the pure, the bold.

Fleeting hopes in shadows we chase,
In a realm of twilight grace.
Softly echoed, laughter's ring,
In the hush where fairies sing.

Petals fall from blossoms rare,
Carried gently by the air.
On this path, where wishes bloom,
Magic lingers, dispelling gloom.

Through the night, enchantments weave,
A tale of joy, we dare believe.
Step with wonder, trust the night,
In the glimmers, find your light.

Shadows of the Sylvan Veil

Beneath the boughs, where secrets hide,
Whispers glide on the evening tide.
Echoes of the forest deep,
In shadows, ancient spirits sleep.

Mossy floors and twilight's breath,
Guard the tales of life and death.
Rays of sunlight trickle through,
Illuminating heart's true view.

A rustle here, a fleeting glance,
In the shadows, spirits dance.
Veils of silence, softly speak,
To those who dare, the brave, the meek.

Underneath the starlit dome,
Nature breathes, forever home.
In every bark and every leaf,
Lies the wisdom, joy, and grief.

So tread with care, the sylvan line,
Where shadows blend and stars align.
In their embrace, find solace near,
A journey bound by love and fear.

Whispers in the Frosted Grove

In the frost of morning's breath,
Nature whispers tales of death.
Frozen branches, lace so fine,
Carrying dreams like scattered pine.

Footfalls soft on crispy ground,
Echoes of a world unbound.
Winter's song, a haunting tune,
With the rise of the pale moon.

Every flake, a gem so bright,
Twinkling softly in the night.
Whispers linger, soft as silk,
In this grove, where shadows milk.

A hush falls, as stillness grows,
Capturing secrets only it knows.
In the cold, warmth still survives,
In the heart, where hope derives.

Beneath the frost, the world awaits,
For spring's embrace, and open gates.
The grove holds stories yet untold,
In whispers, life will soon unfold.

Specters of the Moonlit Glade

In the glade, where shadows churn,
Specters dance, and lanterns burn.
Moonlight spills on wandering souls,
As silence wraps, and night consoles.

Glowing orbs float high above,
Summoning the dreams we love.
Every flicker, every spark,
Guides us gently through the dark.

Footsteps echo, soft and light,
In a realm of pure delight.
Ghostly figures glide with grace,
Weaving through time and space.

The glade holds tales of yore,
Whispers from the days before.
Each encounter, silver threads,
Connecting hearts where memory spreads.

As the night begins to fade,
Hold close the gifts the spirits made.
In the light of dawn, depart,
With specters' love, within your heart.

Luminous Threads of Hidden Realms

In the depths of night's embrace,
Whispers of light take their place,
Weaving tales of dreams once spun,
In realms where time and shadow run.

Stars like stitches in the dark,
Illuminating journeys marked,
Through the fabric of the night,
Where secrets dance in silver light.

Mysteries hold hands with fate,
As twilight bends to the gate,
Of hidden worlds not yet revealed,
By the heart's soft glow, concealed.

Woven threads of stories old,
In each shimmer, a truth unfolds,
Galaxies in twinkling gaze,
Will guide us through the endless maze.

With every breath, the cosmos sighs,
In worlds where the infinite lies,
So we walk with gentle grace,
Embracing all that time can trace.

Twilight Secrets of the Woodland

Beneath the boughs where shadows play,
Twilight whispers of the day,
In the hush of evening's glow,
Nature's secrets start to flow.

Softly tread on mossy ground,
In the quiet, magic's found,
Flickers of the fireflies' dance,
Lead us to a moonlit trance.

Each leaf cradles a tale untold,
Of wanderers brave and bold,
Echoes of the ancients hum,
As the dusk begins to come.

Murmurs blend with the night's caress,
In the woods, we find our rest,
Underneath the starlit dome,
In this sacred place, we roam.

Nature holds her breath so tight,
In the symphony of night,
Whispers cradled in the trees,
The woodland speaks, if just with ease.

Fragments of Celestial Reverie

Up above where shadows wane,
Fragments of dreams begin to reign,
Threaded stars and moonlit beams,
Cradle our most tender dreams.

Galaxies turn in graceful dance,
Calling forth a fateful chance,
Robed in shimmering cosmic hue,
Their stories, ancient yet anew.

With stardust sprinkled on the night,
Whispers of eternity ignite,
Lost in the velvet sky's expanse,
Every twinkle holds a glance.

We ride the currents of the void,
In the vastness, we are buoyed,
Time's tapestry gently weaves,
A space where the heart believes.

Here, in the realm of endless light,
Fragments gather, taking flight,
In celestial reverie's hold,
We find our stories yet untold.

Embracing the Touch of Winter's Mirth

When winter blankets all in white,
The world embraces quiet light,
Where whispers curl in frosty air,
And nature dons a crystal flair.

Softly, snowflakes start to fall,
A gentle hush envelops all,
In every flake, a dance sublime,
Echos of a silver chime.

Branches heavy with their coat,
Mirthful songs begin to float,
Frozen lakes reflect the sun,
In this beauty, we are one.

Hearts aglow with warmth's embrace,
In winter's calm, we find our place,
With every laugh, the cold retreats,
In shared stories, joy repeats.

So let us wander through the snow,
In winter's spell, we'll freely go,
For in this chill, the heart ignites,
Embracing all winter's delights.

Mercury Skies and Winter's Breath

Beneath the silver clouds so light,
The chill of winter greets the night.
Mercury skies, a frozen gleam,
In whispered winds, the world will dream.

The stars like diamonds start to shine,
As frosty breath draws the divine.
Silent echoes dance with grace,
In this enchanted, quiet place.

Each flake a whisper, soft and sweet,
A symphony of cold, discreet.
The moon hangs low, a ghostly pearl,
While winter wraps the earth in twirl.

In twilight's glow, the spirits play,
Their laughter ringing, bright as day.
The mercury skies, a fleeting art,
Awakens warmth within the heart.

So let us walk through twilight's maze,
Where time stands still in silver haze.
Mercury skies and winter's breath,
A canvas draped in nature's depth.

Ethereal Reflections on Icy Mirrors

Upon the lake, a perfect glass,
Where whispers of the past amass.
Ethereal views, a dreamy sight,
Reflecting stars in endless night.

The icy mirrors stir with grace,
Holding secrets of time and space.
Shadows of trees, a ghostly dance,
In every ripple, a fleeting chance.

The cold caress of winter's breath,
A gentle touch that feels like death.
Yet life within the stillness hums,
As nature's pulse quietly drums.

Each glimmering light upon the shore,
Is a memory of what's before.
Ethereal reflections in the dark,
Guide lost souls with hope's small spark.

So let us cherish what we see,
The icy mirrors hold the key.
In every glance, a world reborn,
In winter's grace, we are transformed.

Guardians of the Glimmering Woods

In shadows deep, the guardians stand,
Tall and wise, they grace the land.
Whispers of secrets in the breeze,
They guard the heart of ancient trees.

With branches reaching, twinkling bright,
Their leaves aglow with soft moonlight.
In every rustle, tales unfold,
Of creatures brave, of hearts of gold.

The glimmering woods, alive and true,
Hold echoes of the nights we knew.
Where magic breathes in every hue,
And every heart becomes anew.

The silence speaks with sacred sound,
In this forest where hope is found.
Guardians watch with loving care,
Enfolding all in nature's prayer.

So wander soft through leafy trails,
Where every step a story trails.
In glimmering woods, we find our way,
Guardians of dreams, come what may.

Under the Spell of Frosted Fantasies

Upon the frost, our dreams alight,
Creating shadows in the night.
Frosted fantasies twirl and sway,
In the soft glow of dawn's ballet.

Each crystal formed a tale to tell,
Of winter's kiss, a magic spell.
The world, a canvas, pure and white,
Wrapped in a hush that feels just right.

Snowflakes dance in a swirling waltz,
Blanketing the earth with soft vaults.
In every flake, a whisper clear,
Of hopes and dreams that persevere.

We wander under starlit skies,
Chasing the magic that never dies.
In frosted dreams, our spirits soar,
Finding the peace we've longed for.

So let the fantasies unfold,
In silver light, our hearts behold.
Under the spell of winter's grace,
We find ourselves in time and space.

Ethereal Reflections in a Winter's Gaze

Snowflakes dance like whispered dreams,
Beneath a pale, soft moon's beams.
Each breath a cloud in the frosty air,
Silent echoes of beauty rare.

Trees adorned in crystal lace,
Nature's quiet, serene embrace.
Stars blink above in distant night,
Guiding lost souls with their light.

Footsteps fade on a silver trail,
Stories written in the snow veil.
Time stands still in this tranquil scene,
A world transformed, pure, and serene.

Shadows linger, fading away,
As dawn breaks in shades of gray.
The winter's gaze, a knowing sigh,
Invites the heart to dream and fly.

In this realm where silence sings,
Life pauses, the heart takes wings.
Ethereal whispers fill the space,
Forever held in winter's grace.

Musings of the Frost-Kissed Sylphs

In the hush of the frosty dawn,
Sylphs weave magic, softly drawn.
With laughter light as the drifting snow,
They play where the quiet breezes blow.

Veils of mist, a shimmering sight,
Dancing gleams in the pale moonlight.
Every flake a muse in their flight,
A tapestry spun from the night.

Their whispers echo through the trees,
Carried gently by the winter breeze.
A chorus of voices, soft and clear,
Inviting the world to pause and hear.

Each branch wears a silvery crown,
A kingdom where dreams drift down.
In this realm of frost and light,
Life unfolds in pure delight.

With gentle grace, they roam and play,
Chasing shadows, night turns to day.
In the garden of silence, they roam free,
Frost-kissed sylphs, wild and free.

Tread Lightly on the Enchanted Snow

Step softly on the enchanted snow,
Where the whispers of magic flow.
Each footprint tells a tale untold,
Of secrets hidden, values bold.

Glimmers sparkle in the morning light,
Nature's canvas, pure and bright.
A tapestry of white unfolds,
Where every flake a story holds.

The frosted world breathes soft and slow,
Inviting hearts to wander low.
Amidst the trees, where silence reigns,
The spirit of winter gently entertains.

Beneath the boughs where shadows creep,
Ancient secrets the stillness keeps.
In every silence, a voice shall rise,
To greet the wonder under winter skies.

So tread lightly, feel the grace,
Of enchanted snow, a sacred space.
In every flake, find joy anew,
A whispered dream waiting for you.

Enigma of the Frostbound Fairies

Frostbound fairies in twilight's sigh,
Gleam like stars in the midnight sky.
Their laughter weaves through the icy air,
Mysteries held in the winds of care.

Glistening wings of crystalline light,
Flutter softly in the shadowed night.
Guardians of secrets, soft and kind,
They dance through dreams we leave behind.

With every winter's breath they glide,
In hidden realms, where hopes abide.
Casting spells that sparkle and glow,
They spin the tales of the fallen snow.

In silent corners of a frosty glen,
They gather whispers, time and again.
The enigma of their timeless grace,
Leaves a warm echo in our embrace.

So close your eyes and take a chance,
Join the fairies in their dance.
For in the frost, their magic plays,
A timeless journey in winter's gaze.

Radiant Whimsy of the Sylvan Realm

In forests deep where shadows play,
Colors dance in bright display.
Whispers soft on breezes glide,
Nature's secrets, here they bide.

Amidst the ferns, the sunlight weaves,
Glimmers bright among the leaves.
Sprites and faeries, light as air,
Craft a magic, rare and fair.

The brook hums tunes of olden lore,
As creatures frolic, spirits soar.
Petals twirl in gentle flight,
Celebrating the day's delight.

In twilight's glow, the fireflies gleam,
Casting spells like a waking dream.
Every rustle, every sigh,
Echoes laughter that won't die.

A sylvan realm, in hearts it stays,
Painting life in gentle ways.
With whispers low and breezes warm,
In radiant whimsy, we are reborn.

Illusions in the Starlit Hollow

In the hollow where shadows creep,
Starlight shimmers, secrets steep.
Night's embrace, a velvet cloak,
Silent musings softly spoke.

Illusions dance on moonlit beams,
Gliding through our earthly dreams.
Every flicker, every sigh,
Brought to life beneath the sky.

Whispers trace through ancient trees,
Capturing the night's soft tease.
Wonders twine in silver strands,
Mystical tales from unseen lands.

With every breath, the stars align,
Guiding hearts with their design.
In this place where time stands still,
We find solace, we find will.

In the starlit hollow's gaze,
Enchantment weaves a cosmic maze.
Through bright illusions, we will roam,
In dreams we find our truest home.

The Glow of Hidden Realms

Deeper still, the echoes call,
Through hidden realms, we rise and fall.
Beneath the earth, the glow resides,
Where ancient wisdom gently hides.

Crystals shine in fractured light,
Guiding souls through endless night.
Each heartbeat matches nature's song,
In this glow, we all belong.

Shadows weave a tapestry,
Of stories told by mystery.
Every whisper, every sigh,
Unraveling within the sky.

In twilight's mist, the secrets blend,
Where beginnings and endings mend.
Here, beneath the surface dream,
The glow of worlds begins to gleam.

These hidden realms, a treasure vast,
Where echoes of our past are cast.
In every shadow, in every light,
A glow eternal shines so bright.

Chasing Phantoms Through Silver Frost

In winter's breath, a crisp expanse,
Phantoms dance in frosty trance.
Silver threads on velvet nights,
Chasing dreams in glimmering lights.

Whispers echo through the air,
Haunting tales of those who dare.
With each step, the frost will creak,
In chilly silence, shadows speak.

Through the woods, the echoes roam,
Guiding spirits back to home.
In the mist, their laughter swirls,
Chasing phantoms, lost in twirls.

Frosty patterns paint the ground,
In this world where dreams are found.
Underneath the moon's soft glow,
Through silver frost, our spirits flow.

As dawn approaches, shadows fade,
But memories of phantoms stayed.
Through the chill, we keep them near,
In the heart, they reappear.

Shivering Lights Beneath the Sky's Tapestry

Stars flicker and dance in the night,
Swirling whispers of dreams take flight.
The breeze carries tales from afar,
Guiding the heart like a brightening star.

Each glow paints a story untold,
In hues of silver and threads of gold.
They shiver like secrets on the line,
Illuminating paths where shadows intertwine.

Waves of light ripple through the dark,
Awakening echoes, igniting a spark.
Beneath the sky's vast, endless dome,
We find our courage as we search for home.

In silence we linger, gazing above,
Wrapped in the blanket of twilight's glove.
Each twinkling promise, a gentle sigh,
Invites us to wonder, to dream, and to fly.

O glimmering lights, so bittersweet,
With you, our solitude finds its beat.
We cherish your magic, never to part,
As the universe whispers into our heart.

Mystical Glimmers of Faery Light

In the forest where shadows weave,
There dance the faeries, dreams to believe.
Glimmers sparkle like dew on leaves,
Whispers of magic are all that it weaves.

Underneath boughs of ancient trees,
Soft laughter echoes with the breeze.
They flit like fragments of a lost song,
Guiding the wanderers who've roamed too long.

Beneath the glow of twilight's hue,
The path unfolds like a secret view.
With shimmer in their eyes, they twirl,
Inviting souls to join their whirl.

Adorned in colors, a radiant flight,
They beckon softly, a luring light.
In the stillness, we feel their grace,
Carried on whispers, we find our place.

With each flicker, enchantments reveal,
Stories of wonder that time cannot steal.
In this realm where dreams take flight,
We lose our hearts to faery light.

Shadows that Sing Beneath the Moon

Under the gaze of the silvery sphere,
Shadows emerge, no longer a fear.
They dance and sway in a melodic tune,
Echoing secrets beneath the moon.

In quiet corners where stillness resides,
The night unveils its magical guides.
With voices soft, they call your name,
Binding the heart in a gentle frame.

Each note ripples through the dark,
A lullaby woven, a lingering spark.
In the tender glow, they come alive,
Breathing in the dreams that we strive.

Shadows entwined, weaving their tale,
In whispered rhythms, they softly exhale.
The night grows deeper, our worries depart,
Melodies weaving through the heart.

Together we sway in ephemeral light,
Caught in the magic of the endless night.
With shadows that sing, we drift and glide,
Finding our solace on this moonlit ride.

Ice Crystals and Mythic Whispers

In the stillness where winter reigns,
Ice crystals fall, left on the plains.
They glimmer like diamonds under the sun,
Whispers of myths that cannot be spun.

Each flake tells a tale from yore,
Of ancient lands and the legends they bore.
In their silent shimmer, a magic resides,
Inviting us closer to where dreamland abides.

As frost weaves its lace upon the trees,
The world becomes hushed, carried by ease.
Whispers entwined in the chill of the night,
Guide us through shadows, illuminating light.

With every heartbeat, the frost will hum,
Echoing stories of where we came from.
In these whispers wrapped in delicate glass,
We discover the moments that quietly pass.

So let us wander in winter's embrace,
Through icy realms, we find our place.
With crystals that sparkle and secrets to find,
We dance with the whispers that nature has signed.

The Light of Wishes in Winter's Veil

In the hush of night so deep,
Ice-crystals in silence keep.
Wishes whisp'ring on the breeze,
Glimmers caught in silver trees.

Candles flicker, softly dance,
Under frost's enchanting trance.
Hearts entwined in love's embrace,
Seeking warmth in winter's grace.

Dreams ignite like stars above,
Wrapped in warmth from hope and love.
Each breath a promise, brave and bright,
Guiding souls through the night.

Veils of snow, a magic shroud,
Whispers float, both soft and loud.
Cloaked in wonder, we take flight,
Together, hearts aglow with light.

Crafting Dreams with Ice-kissed Grace

With each flake, a story spun,
Silhouettes where dreams have run.
Canvas blank, yet spirits soar,
Creating worlds we all adore.

Shapes of crystal intertwine,
Beauty crafted, oh so fine.
Fragile visions, caught in time,
Chasing echoes, soft and prime.

Hands that mold the winter's charm,
Each gentle touch, a heart's warm calm.
Mysteries wrapped in frosty lace,
Unfolding joys in frozen space.

A dance of light, a breath so clear,
In winter's grasp, we hold what's dear.
Moments fleeting, yet they stay,
In dreams we weave, come what may.

The Frost's Lure in Faery Lanterns

Glimmers shine in twilight's glow,
Frosted paths where whispers flow.
Faery lights that softly lure,
Secrets held in night's allure.

Beneath the stars, shadows sway,
Echoes of the fae at play.
Frosted wishes on a stream,
Guided forth by hopes that beam.

In the stillness, tales unfold,
Of ancient love and dreams retold.
Lanterns guiding through the dark,
Igniting all with magic's spark.

Nature's breath a canvas wide,
Where hearts dance, and dreams abide.
In the frost, a warm embrace,
Filling voids with light and grace.

Where the Stars Meet Glistening Dew

A tapestry of night so bright,
Stars are jewels in the flight.
Dewdrops sparkle on the grass,
In silence, whisper dreams that pass.

Morn awakens, soft and true,
Nature's breath, a spark anew.
Gentle glimmers kiss the dawn,
Promises of a world reborn.

Underneath a velvet sky,
Silhouettes of dreams nearby.
Each moment, fleeting yet profound,
In stillness, magic can be found.

Where the stars and dewdrops meet,
Life's melody is pure and sweet.
In their union, hopes align,
Crafting dreams through space and time.

Silhouettes of Light Beneath the Ice

Beneath the ice, the shadows play,
A dance of light, in cold array.
Reflections gleam, a soft embrace,
In stillness whispers, winter's grace.

Eerie forms glide through the deep,
Silent secrets that they keep.
Frosty edges frame the scene,
Mysteries lost, yet keenly seen.

Twilight's breath, a tender sigh,
As twinkling stars light up the sky.
Beneath the chill, the heart will glow,
In frozen realms, where dreamers go.

Shadows shift in crystal light,
Beneath the ice, the world feels right.
A symphony of peace, so pure,
In this stillness, our hearts endure.

Each silhouette tells a tale,
Of whispered winds that never fail.
In icy depths, we seek our dreams,
In fleeting dance, where stillness beams.

Shimmering Wishes Among the Hills

Amidst the hills, where wishes soar,
A shimmering light at every door.
Soft murmurs dance on gentle air,
Hopes woven in the fabric rare.

Underneath the cloak of night,
Stars twinkle with a hopeful light.
Each wish cast, a silver thread,
In moonlit glades, the dreams are spread.

Echoes cradle the secrets kept,
In nature's arms, our hearts are swept.
Shimmering paths through shadows wind,
With every step, new hopes we find.

Whispers lift on breezes sweet,
In every heartbeat, a rhythmic beat.
Among the hills, our spirits soar,
As wishes spark like never before.

Together we gather, hand in hand,
In shimmering wishes, we take a stand.
Among the hills, our stories blend,
In this enchanted space, where dreams transcend.

Frosty Kisses on Fairy Wings

Upon the breeze, the fairies fly,
With frosty kisses, they brush the sky.
Whispers twinkle in moonlit glow,
A soft enchantment, a tale to sow.

Glistening wings like winter's breath,
Spreading joy, defying death.
In frosty realms where magic calls,
Fairy laughter in the starlit halls.

Each gentle touch a snowflake's dance,
A fleeting moment, a wondrous chance.
Through frozen night, their echoes ring,
Crafting dreams with every swing.

As dawn approaches, the magic fades,
But frosty kisses linger in shades.
In hidden corners, the fairies beam,
Leaving traces of a waking dream.

With every flutter, hope ignites,
In frosty kisses, the heart unites.
A world of wonder just out of view,
Where fairies roam and dreams come true.

Light-Songs of the Winter Grove

In winter's grove, the light-songs play,
A gentle melody, soft as day.
Whispers weave through branches bare,
An echo of warmth in the frosty air.

Each note a flake, unique and bright,
Dancing down with the soft moonlight.
In the hush of snow, the songs arise,
Beneath the stars, beneath the skies.

Glistening paths where shadows roam,
In every heart, a place called home.
The winter grove, a sacred space,
Where voices blend in a timeless grace.

Frosted branches hold the tune,
Beneath the watchful, silver moon.
The light-songs echo, pure and clear,
Within this grove, we draw near.

A symphony of peace we find,
In winter's grasp, our spirits bind.
In light-songs shared, we come alive,
In winter's grove, our hopes revive.

Whispers of Luminous Shadows

In the still of night, a whisper calls,
Secrets cloaked in shadowed halls.
Moonlight dances on the ground,
Silent echoes all around.

Ghostly figures drift and sway,
Where forgotten dreams decay.
Hints of laughter, soft and light,
Guide the lost through endless night.

Rustling leaves sing ancient lore,
While shadows creep to close the door.
A moment captured, time stands still,
In whispers of the wind's soft trill.

Through the gloom, the spirits glide,
Carried forth by the turning tide.
In this realm, they weave and spin,
The stories of what might have been.

So linger here, oh heart so brave,
In the embrace of twilight's wave.
Find the magic, let it flow,
In whispers where the wild hearts go.

Enchanted Dreams in Frosted Glades

In glades where frost and magic meet,
Whispers twirl on silent feet.
Dreams of wonder, soft and bright,
Glimmer gently in the night.

Snowflakes dance on silver beams,
Weaving together our hidden dreams.
In every corner, a story glows,
In the heart of winter's prose.

Beneath the trees, a world so rare,
Frozen secrets linger in the air.
As starlight kisses, the cold cascades,
We lose ourselves in frosted glades.

Awake the magic, let it soar,
With every heartbeat, we restore.
The beauty held in icy streams,
In enchanted paths of winter dreams.

So wander forth, where spirits play,
Through frosted glades, let shadows sway.
With every step, be brave and free,
In the timeless dance of reverie.

Glimmers of the Ethereal Veil

Beyond the curtain of the night,
Lies a world bathed in soft light.
Whispers brush the edges near,
Glimmers of joy, free from fear.

Through the mist, the figures gleam,
Caught in an everlasting dream.
Each shimmer carried on the breeze,
Secrets told by ancient trees.

A fleeting glance, a fleeting sound,
In this realm, lost souls are found.
Silken threads weave through the air,
Bind us close, though unaware.

In twilight's kiss, the shadows blend,
Where beginnings meet to find an end.
Echoes shimmer, memories sail,
In the glimmers of the ethereal veil.

So join the dance with heart unveiled,
In the light where dreams have sailed.
Feel the magic, let it thrive,
In realms where only dreams survive.

Dances of Light on Crystal Leaves

In the forest where the sunlight weaves,
You can find the crystal leaves.
Sparkling bright in the gentle sway,
Nature's dance upon display.

Dappled rays through branches play,
As shadows chase the light away.
Each leaf a prism, bold and bright,
Twinkling softly with sheer delight.

Underneath the canopy's grace,
Every step finds its sacred place.
With each rustle, a gentle tease,
As whispers flow on the crisp breeze.

So breathe it in, the beauty near,
In dappled light, let go of fear.
Embrace the magic that nature gives,
In dances of light where wonder lives.

Together we weave, forever spun,
On crystal leaves, beneath the sun.
In every moment, life and dreams,
Shine forever in silken beams.

Secrets of the Moonlit Clearings

In the hush of night, shadows play,
Stars whisper tales in a silvery sway.
Each leaf dances lightly, the breeze a sigh,
Secrets of dreams beneath the sky.

Gentle light spills through branches wide,
Guiding lost souls like a soft tide.
Echoes of laughter drift on the hue,
Moonlit clearings hold stories anew.

Twisting pathways lead hearts to roam,
Where wanderers find a place called home.
Under the gaze of the watchful moon,
Life's fleeting moments, a sweet tune.

In every rustle, in every call,
Nature weaves magic, enchanting all.
With every breath, a promise is sealed,
In moonlit clearings, souls are healed.

Glowing Echoes in the Winter Mist

Pale shadows dance in the frost-kissed air,
Whispers of winter weave everywhere.
Gentle echoes in the quiet night,
Leading the heart with their soft light.

Through the mist, a path softly glows,
Painting the world where the cool wind blows.
Silent footsteps on crisp, fallen leaves,
Swaying branches in delicate weaves.

A blanket of white, so tender and pure,
Cocooning the earth in a dreamlike lure.
Stars above twinkle like distant dreams,
Glowing echoes whispering in moonbeams.

In the stillness, hearts begin to thaw,
As nature reveals its wondrous law.
In winter's embrace, we find our way,
Glowing echoes guide, come what may.

Guardian Spirits in Dappled Light

In forests deep, where the shadows blend,
Guardian spirits weave and bend.
Sunlight dapples through the leafy screen,
Mystic beings weave a tale unseen.

Watchful eyes in the twilight's embrace,
Guiding the wanderer through time and space.
A flicker of light, then nothing but air,
Guardian spirits always near, always there.

Among the ferns, whispers of trees,
Ancient stories carried by the breeze.
With each rustle, a promise is kept,
In dappled light, the forest has slept.

Echoes of laughter, soft, like a sigh,
Calling the dreamers who wish to fly.
In the heart of the woods, they thrive and play,
Guardian spirits, lighting the way.

Twinkling Secrets Among the Pines

In a grove where the tall pines sing,
Twinkling secrets on gossamer wing.
Softly they flutter, elusive and bright,
Guiding lost souls through the silent night.

Each sigh of the wind tells a tale to remember,
Secrets of warmth in the chill of December.
Beneath their boughs, shadows intertwine,
Whispered promises in the soft incline.

Glimmers of hope in the moonlit glen,
Reminders of love from afar again.
With every twinkle, a star's gentle plea,
Among the pines, we feel so free.

The night unveils a magical embrace,
In secretive whispers, we find our place.
Twinkling secrets among nature's design,
In the heart of the forest, mysteries align.

Veils of Illumination in the Shimmering Night

Beneath the stars, a whisper glows,
Shimmering light through shadows flows.
Each breath a secret, softly spun,
Veils of night reveal the dawn.

In silken folds, dreams take their flight,
Guided by ghosts of silver light.
The moon, a lantern, bright and bold,
Illuminates the tales of old.

Crickets sing a lullaby tune,
As fireflies dance 'neath the gentle moon.
Weights of burdens drift in the air,
Veils of magic linger with care.

The world above, a canvas bright,
Strokes of beauty in the night.
Each flicker tells a story shared,
In the glow, lost hearts are bared.

As dawn approaches, shadows flee,
Leaving behind a memory,
For in the quiet, truths ignited,
Veils of illumination, forever lighted.

Frosted Glimmers in the Enchanted Thicket

In the woods where silence sleeps,
Frosted glimmers, nature keeps.
Icicles hang from branches bare,
Whispers of winter fill the air.

Through the thicket, shadows play,
Crisp and cold, the light will sway.
Each step a crunch on frosted ground,
Magic lingers, all around.

Footprints lead to secret places,
Where time holds still and nature graces.
Glistening dew begins to shine,
In this enchanted realm, divine.

Echoes of a gentle breeze,
Carry tales through leafless trees.
Frosted sparkles, a fleeting sight,
In the stillness, winter's light.

As stars fade with the coming day,
Nature's beauty fades away.
Yet in the heart, the memory stays,
Frosted glimmers, lost in haze.

Dreams Woven in the Chilled Air

In the coolness of twilight's breath,
Dreams are spun, defying death.
Threads of hope, in the chilled air,
Whispered wishes, light as prayer.

Clouds drift by, a canvas vast,
Painting futures, shadows cast.
Each moment woven, hearts entwine,
In the fabric of dreams divine.

Stars emerge, bold and bright,
Guiding paths through endless night.
A tapestry of thoughts and schemes,
Laced together with secret dreams.

In the stillness, visions bloom,
Casting spells, dispelling gloom.
The chilled air beckons, soft and fair,
Holding dreams that linger there.

As dawn brings light to fading schemes,
Threads unspool from tangled dreams.
Yet in the heart, they linger near,
Woven in the chilled air's cheer.

Hues of Forgotten Magic

In twilight's glow, colors blend,
Hues of magic that never end.
Whispers of a world unseen,
Vibrant shades of what has been.

Through tangled woods, the colors weave,
Stories of those who dared believe.
Each leaf a tale, each blossom bright,
Hues of magic dance in the light.

Crimson, sapphire, emerald dreams,
Flow like water, passion streams.
Forgotten spells in every hue,
Their power lingers, pure and true.

As shadows lengthen, colors play,
Fleeting forms in the fading day.
In fading light, the spirits cling,
Hues of magic in the spring.

With night's embrace, the colors fade,
Leaving behind the dreams we made.
Yet deep within, their essence stays,
Hues of forgotten magic's ways.

Starlit Paths of the Woodland Spirits

In shadows deep where silence breathes,
The woodland whispers softly weaves.
Beneath the stars, the spirits dance,
A fleeting glimpse, a dreamlike chance.

Through ancient trees their laughter rings,
As night unveils her secret wings.
They guide the lost with glimmering light,
And paint the dark with emerald bright.

Their voices echo in the wood,
A serenade, a magical mood.
In every breeze, their stories flow,
A melody only night can know.

With every step on mossy ground,
The spirits twirl, a sight profound.
Thy wandering heart shall find its way,
With woodland friends till break of day.

So tread with care, and listen close,
For in the dark, they are engrossed.
You'll find the peace that nature lends,
On starlit paths where magic bends.

Twilight's Embrace of Elysian Whispers

The twilight drapes in silken hues,
A canvas drawn of greens and blues.
With every breath, the silence sways,
In Elysium, where fortune plays.

The whispers dance on twilight's breath,
A tranquil song that hints of death.
Yet in this grace, the beauty lies,
In fleeting time, the spirit flies.

With gentle rays that kiss the ground,
The echoes of the lost are found.
In every flicker, hope remains,
A tapestry of joy and pains.

Beneath the stars, the stories grow,
Of heroes past and love's soft glow.
In twilight's arms, the heart shall soar,
To find the peace that's known before.

So linger here, and seek the grace,
Within the dusk, a warm embrace.
For life is but a fleeting sigh,
In twilight's arms, we learn to fly.

Glimmers of the Otherworldly Frost

When winter's reign casts diamond light,
The earth is dressed in purest white.
Each flake a whisper from the skies,
A message wrapped, where silence lies.

Beneath the frost, the dreams do dwell,
In icy realms, they weave a spell.
With glimmers bright, the spirits twine,
Embracing all that sparkles fine.

The trees, adorned in sparkling lace,
Invite the world to slow its pace.
In every corner, magic thrives,
Where winter's breath in stillness strives.

The moonlight plays on icy streams,
As nature hums her quiet dreams.
In every shimmer, stories spun,
Of battles fought and countless won.

So tread with care on glittered ground,
For in the chill, enchantments abound.
With every step, a tale unfurls,
In this frost-bound realm of hidden pearls.

Revelations of the Chiming Breeze

In gentle winds, the secrets sigh,
A choir soft beneath the sky.
The breeze, a friend that guides and sings,
Of hidden truths that nature brings.

With every note, the world awakes,
The whispers weave as daylight breaks.
From leaves and flowers, tales arise,
In every gust, a sweet surprise.

Through fields and valleys, far and wide,
The chiming breeze does not abide.
It dances low and rises high,
A messenger from earth to sky.

In every breath, the stories blend,
Of ancient wisdom that will mend.
Embrace the wind, let it reveal,
The truths that time cannot conceal.

So listen close and set your mind,
To all the wonders left behind.
In chiming notes, the world does flow,
A tapestry of love to grow.

Beacons in the Midnight Wood

In shadows deep where silence dwells,
The whispers dance, the forest tells.
Each flicker bright, a guiding spark,
To light the way through endless dark.

Beneath the boughs, the spirits play,
In twilight's grip, they weave their sway.
A mystery wrapped in moonlit air,
Where dreams take flight without a care.

The river sings a haunting tune,
While starlit skies unveil the moon.
Soft rustling leaves join in the beat,
A serenade so pure and sweet.

With every step on ancient ground,
The heartbeat of the wood resounds.
In this embrace, time slips away,
As night unfolds a grand ballet.

So wander here, let worries cease,
Find solace in this night's release.
In beacons' glow, your heart shall soar,
The midnight wood holds secrets more.

Echoes of Enchantment in the Snow

In blankets white, the silence reigns,
Each flake a whisper, soft and plain.
Beneath the stars, a world aglow,
Where dreams are cast in purest snow.

The branches bow with crystal lace,
As nature dons its frozen grace.
In every drift, a story lies,
Of winter's charm beneath the skies.

Footprints trace a path anew,
In sparkles bright of silver hue.
The frosty air holds magic's breath,
In echoes soft of warmth and death.

A hush descends, the night draws near,
With every sound, enchantment's near.
As shadows stretch and moonlight glows,
The world awaits what beauty shows.

So linger here, let wonder reign,
In snowy lands, free of pain.
Embrace the night, let spirits roam,
In echoes sweet, forever home.

Shimmering Fantasies of the Frostbound Grove

In glimmers bright, the grove awakes,
With frostbound beauty, silence quakes.
Each branch adorned in icy sheen,
A world transformed, a chilling dream.

Beneath the frost, the earth does breathe,
Where fantasies and wishes weave.
In every crystal, stories spin,
Of whispered hopes and loves within.

The moonlight kisses every tree,
In shimmering grace, they long to be.
With every sigh of winter's night,
The grove enchants with soft delight.

Among the shadows, magic flows,
As nature's pulse begins to glow.
With every breath, a dream takes flight,
In frostbound realms of purest white.

So wander deep, let hearts ignite,
In fantasies, where stars are bright.
Embrace the chill, the gleaming sight,
In frostbound groves, love finds its light.

Enchanted Paths Through Crystal Glades

Through crystal glades the pathway winds,
With every step, a treasure finds.
The trees like giants, proud and tall,
Whisper secrets, heed their call.

In sunlight's grace, the dew does gleam,
A carpet laid for dreams to dream.
With gentle hands, the breeze does weave,
A tapestry that bids us leave.

The songs of birds on high take flight,
In purest joy, they greet the light.
Each glade a haven, pure and bright,
Where hearts may dance in sheer delight.

With every turn, the magic grows,
In whispers soft, the forest knows.
The path unfolds, a tale of old,
In crystal light, new dreams are told.

So wander forth, let spirit soar,
Through crystal glades, seek out the lore.
In every step, let wonder guide,
In enchanted paths, forever bide.

Melodies of the Frost-kissed Grove

Whispers dance upon the breeze,
As winter weaves her soft refrain,
Branches glisten, bending with ease,
Nature sings in cold domain.

Footfalls echo on crystal ground,
Snowflakes twirl, a graceful show,
In the silence, beauty found,
Life's lullaby begins to flow.

Moonlight kisses every bough,
Stars peek through the frosty air,
Time stands still, a solemn vow,
The grove holds secrets, rich and rare.

In this realm of chill and grace,
Each note rings true, a heartfelt song,
The magic of this frozen place,
Invites the dreamers to belong.

So let the melodies ascend,
Through frozen paths where spirits glide,
In the frost-kissed grove, my friend,
We find our hearts and souls collide.

The Glinting Path of Dreamweavers

Underneath the twilight's glow,
Glimmers lead us through the night,
Whispers of the dreamers flow,
Crafting visions, pure delight.

Luminous the stars will shine,
Guiding footsteps soft and slow,
Threads of fate, a design divine,
Through the shadows, secrets grow.

Winding trails of silver light,
Where the weary hearts take flight,
In the hush, dreams intertwine,
Revealing futures, glowing bright.

With each step, the night unfolds,
A tapestry of hopes and fears,
Stories whispered, gently told,
Echoes linger through the years.

So follow the glinting way,
As dreamweavers spin their art,
In the magic of the gray,
We discover every heart.

Nightfall's Embrace on Shimmering Wings

As daylight fades to dusky hue,
Softly wraps the world in sleep,
Nightfall's embrace, tender and true,
Hushes secrets that we keep.

Owls call softly in the night,
While shadows stretch and softly sway,
On shimmering wings, they take flight,
Dancing dreams to guide the way.

Stars awaken in the deep,
Their twinkling tales of ancient lore,
Across the sky, where visions leap,
Night unveils what hearts adore.

Cooler winds begin to sigh,
Rustling leaves in whispered tone,
In the stillness, hopes will fly,
To places yet to be known.

So take a breath, let worries cease,
In night's embrace, find your wings,
With every heartbeat, feel the peace,
As magic in the darkness sings.

Secretive Lanterns in the Woodland

Tucked away where shadows lie,
Lanterns flicker, soft and bright,
Secrets whispered by the sigh,
Of ancient trees in gentle night.

Each glow reveals a hidden tale,
Of creatures bold and spirits free,
Through winding paths, we search and sail,
To find the heart of mystery.

Softly glowing, they lead the way,
In the dark, their warmth ignites,
Through tangled roots and leaves of gray,
We wander towards enchanted sights.

In the woodland's hush, time slows,
Every flicker holds a wish,
Magic flows where the wild rose grows,
An endless, loving, secret swish.

So linger 'neath the starry dome,
Embrace the stories in the glade,
For in this place, you're never alone,
With secretive lanterns light your way.

Faery Sparkles in a Silver Mist

In the twilight's gentle breath,
Faeries weave the light they dress.
Sparkles twinkle, soft and bright,
In the embrace of the night.

Whispers dance on silver streams,
Painting hues of fleeting dreams.
Cloaked in magic, they sway and swirl,
Inviting all to join their whirl.

Glimmers rise from dewy glades,
Casting spells in soft cascades.
Nature's lull, a symphony,
Echoes through eternity.

Beneath the stars' watchful eyes,
The faery realm in beauty lies.
Holding secrets of the breeze,
In their laughter, hearts find ease.

The Ephemeral Dance of Winter Spirits

In the hush of falling snow,
Winter spirits weave and flow.
Frosty breath in sparkling air,
Dancing lightly, without care.

Moonlight gilds the icy ground,
In this realm where peace is found.
Twinkling stars mark their ballet,
As shadows gently drift away.

Silent whispers through the trees,
Mighty echoes in the freeze.
Each heartbeat, a fleeting chance,
To join the spirits in their dance.

Moments fleeting, yet profound,
Nature's magic all around.
As winter fades, they fade too,
Yet in dreams will still break through.

Secrets Unveiled in Glacial Dreams

Beneath the surface cold and deep,
Ancient secrets subtly seep.
In glacial dreams where whispers play,
Time stands still, night turns to day.

Crystalline visions, pure and bright,
Unlock the shadows of the night.
Each fragment holds a tale untold,
Of magic woven from the cold.

Silent echoes call and sigh,
As the frost begins to cry.
Voices dance in frozen streams,
Delivering their haunting themes.

A world revealed from icy shroud,
Ensnared within a silken cloud.
In the stillness, hearts align,
Finding solace in the divine.

The Shimmer of Hidden Fairytales

In the heart of ancient woods,
Where every tree has understood,
Shimmering echoes of the past,
Whispered tales that hold us fast.

Mushrooms glow in twilight's glow,
Guarding secrets we might know.
Every path a story's breath,
Life and magic, victory and death.

When shadows cast their gentle veil,
The fairytales begin to sail.
Elders speak of love and fear,
Of every joy, each hidden tear.

Underneath the silver moon,
Ancient melodies find their tune.
In the quiet, stories shine,
Tales of wonder intertwined.

Gleams of Magic Under Snowy Boughs

Under branches thick with snow,
The silver shadows dance and glow.
Whispers weave through icy air,
While dreams of wonder linger there.

Footprints lead to realms of light,
Where spirits twirl in frosty flight.
Glimmers of joy, pure and bright,
Invite the heart to take to flight.

Crystals form on every leaf,
Binding joy, dispelling grief.
The cold embraces warmth inside,
A magical, enchanting ride.

With each flake that softly falls,
Nature's beauty gently calls.
In this world of winter's might,
Gleams of magic spark delight.

So take a moment, breathe it in,
Let the magic's song begin.
Under snowy boughs so high,
A universe, where dreams can fly.

The Frosty Whisper of Forgotten Realms

In the hush of winter's breath,
Echoes of a world, like death.
Whispers drift through aged trees,
Stories carried on the breeze.

Shadows cast by moonlight pale,
Reveal secrets where dreams sail.
Frosty tales, both dark and bright,
Come alive in the still night.

The silence holds a magic deep,
Guarding visions, lost in sleep.
Every flake a story spun,
From the past, where all begun.

Listen close, the echoes call,
Ancient voices rise and fall.
In this realm, time has no bound,
Frosty whispers all around.

So let the night embrace your heart,
Feel the magic never part.
For in the frost, the tales unveil,
A journey through forgotten trails.

Enigmas of the Moonlit Glade

In the glade where shadows play,
Moonlight dances, bright as day.
Mysteries weave through the night,
Whispers glow with silver light.

Every stone and leaf a tale,
Beneath the stars, the breezes sail.
Enigmas spark, the heart ignites,
In the stillness of the nights.

Branches sway with secrets low,
Lost in dreams that drift and flow.
Nature wraps her arms around,
The magic in this sacred ground.

With each breath, the wonders rise,
Softly kissed by moonlit skies.
In the glade where shadows blend,
Eternal tales that never end.

So wandering souls, heed the call,
In moonlit glades, we find it all.
Enigmas wrapped in starlit grace,
A timeless journey, we embrace.

Frosted Dreams in Hidden Hollows

In hidden hollows, dreams unfold,
Wrapped in frost, and tales retold.
Nature's breath on softest ground,
Where magic whispers, all around.

Glimmers twinkle on the ice,
Each a star, pure and precise.
Silent secrets lie in wait,
For wandering hearts who contemplate.

Winds of winter gently sigh,
Carrying dreams that soar and fly.
Through the woods, the stories roam,
In frosted dreams, we find a home.

Every flake a wish divine,
In the hollows, stars align.
A tapestry of white and gold,
In nature's grasp, our spirits hold.

So, spend a moment, lost in time,
In hidden hollows, feel the rhyme.
Frosted dreams, our hearts embrace,
A fleeting glimpse of winter's grace.

Breaths of Enchantment in Winter's Grip

In the hush of a silver day,
Snowflakes twirl, a ballet of gray.
Trees wear lace, their branches bend,
Whispers of dreams that never end.

Footprints lead where shadows play,
A world transformed, in soft array.
Glistening crystals catch the light,
In winter's hold, all feels right.

Breath of chill upon the air,
Silent secrets everywhere.
Frost-kissed whispers, magic told,
In the heart where warmth unfolds.

Beneath the sky, a canvas white,
Stars emerge in the gathering night.
In the quiet, hope ignites,
Winter's charm in peaceful sights.

As twilight drapes its velvet hue,
Enchanted moments, deep and true.
In every breath, a spell we weave,
Winter's charm makes us believe.

Luminous Stories of the Frosted Woods

In the woods where shadows glide,
Golden moonlight, trees abide.
Frosted whispers fill the air,
Each step taken with tender care.

Branches glisten, secrets sway,
Nature's tales in bright array.
Footfalls soft on frozen ground,
In these woods, true magic found.

Pine and birch in moonlit dance,
Sparkling paths, an endless chance.
Stories spun in winter's breath,
Life and memory intertwine, death.

Luminous tales beneath the stars,
Whispers heard from near and far.
Time stands still within this realm,
The heart of nature at the helm.

In every corner, charm resides,
Hidden wonders, nature guides.
Frosted woods, enchanting sight,
Stories wake with the night light.

The Silent Flicker of Hidden Magic

In shadows deep, where dreams reside,
Flickering flickers, magic's guide.
Softly whispered, a secret plea,
In the heart, where none can see.

Through thickened mist, the silence grows,
Ancient tales the forest knows.
Every spark, a star reborn,
In the stillness, hope is worn.

Gentle breath of the midnight air,
Unseen wonders everywhere.
Life awakens, in moments small,
A secret dance in the nightfall.

In the dark, where colors blend,
Magic waits, around the bend.
A flicker here, a shimmer there,
Silent stories, weaved with care.

Each heartbeat echoes, soft and clear,
Whispers of magic, ever near.
In the night, we find our spark,
Hidden magic in the dark.

Twilight's Grace in Frosted Den

Twilight dances on the snow,
Softest hues begin to glow.
In the den where shadows creep,
Winter's secrets, soft and deep.

Frosted boughs in gentle weep,
Nature's lullaby, quiet, sweet.
Under stars, a fleeting glance,
Whispers in a frosty trance.

Moonlit paths with silver sheen,
Each step taken, calm and keen.
In this den where magic sways,
Time stands still in soft arrays.

Embrace the hush, the world in peace,
In winter's grip, we find release.
Twilight's grace, a tender kiss,
Frosted dreams, a world of bliss.

Within the night, soft shadows play,
As twilight fades, the stars convey.
In this frosted den, we find,
A sacred space, of heart and mind.

Shards of Light in Twilight's Grasp

Twilight weaves its gentle thread,
Fractured beams of gold and red.
Whispers float on evening's sigh,
As shadows stretch and softly die.

Stars emerge with gleaming eyes,
Guardians of the velvet skies.
A dance of hues, a fleeting grace,
In this moment, time finds its place.

The world within begins to fade,
Where dreams and secrets softly wade.
In twilight's grasp, all hearts ignite,
With shards of hope, we chase the light.

Echoes linger in the night,
As day gives way to soft twilight.
Each flicker speaks of stories deep,
In quiet realms where shadows creep.

Celebrate the colors bright,
That shimmer softly, pure delight.
In twilight's arms, let spirits soar,
In scattered light, we crave for more.

Dreaming in the Silence of the Frost

In winter's hush, the world retreats,
A blanket white, where silence meets.
In crystal dreams, the shadows play,
While night unfolds a cold ballet.

Each breath a cloud, each step a sigh,
As frosty stars blink in the sky.
The moon whispers secrets long and old,
In silver light, the dreams unfold.

Echoes of laughter dance on air,
In frozen realms beyond compare.
A world untouched by time's cruel hand,
Where wishes weave like grains of sand.

In stillness deep, we chase the dawn,
A tapestry of frost is drawn.
As nature sighs in tranquil light,
We find our dreams in winter's night.

Awaken to the morning's glow,
Where every flake begins to show.
In silence wrapped, our hearts now trust,
Dreaming in the frost's soft hush.

Celestial Dances of the Twilight Fey

Beneath the boughs of ancient trees,
Where whispers ride on evening breeze.
Fey creatures twirl in mystic trance,
In twilight's glow, they weave and dance.

Glimmers spark in the softening light,
As stars awaken from their flight.
The air alive with laughter sweet,
In harmony, their rhythms meet.

Each swirl ignites the dusky haze,
With glimmers bright and endless praise.
Celestial realms lift spirits high,
Above, beneath the twilight sky.

A symphony of soft delight,
In shadows born of soft twilight.
The fey unite in grand display,
To guide the night and greet the day.

Magic swirls in the fading grace,
Of twilight's arms, an endless space.
With each step, a story spun,
In dances bright, all hearts are won.

The Lure of Faery Light amidst Shadows

In the dark where whispers creep,
Faery lights begin to leap.
Dancing softly, like a flame,
Each flicker calls, yet none to tame.

Amidst the shadows, secrets play,
In glimmers bright, they lead astray.
A beckoning in every glow,
The lure of night begins to show.

Lost in dreams, we chase the spark,
That leads us deep within the dark.
With every step, a tale unwinds,
A tapestry the fey designed.

Mysterious voices sing so sweet,
Where earth and sky in twilight meet.
The faeries guide with silent grace,
In hidden paths, we find our place.

A world awakened, woven tight,
In the embrace of shadowed light.
With every heartbeat, souls ignite,
The lure of faery, pure delight.

www.ingramcontent.com/pod-product-compliance
Ingram Content Group UK Ltd.
Pitfield, Milton Keynes, MK11 3LW, UK
UKHW021430160125
4146UKWH00006B/54

9 781805 594703